FAITHFUL SERVICE

FAITHFUL SERVICE

Encouragement for those working behind the scenes

Rich Chaffin

ISBN: 1500837520
ISBN 13: 9781500837525

Table of Contents

1

Faithful

Things don't always go the way we want. You have made a strong commitment to do the right thing, the loving thing, but somehow the results of that decision have left you confused and frustrated. Will you continue to be faithful? Or will you give in to these thoughts of compromise that make so much sense to you now that things are difficult?

What happens when the people I am serving disrespect me, acting with a sense of entitlement? Or what will I do when I have that painful feeling that those in authority are using me and my fellow servants, taking advantage of our passion and heart to serve?

The message of this little book is for those who want to be faithful. You started well and you want to finish strong. But you have also become keenly aware of the realities of a life of service. It seems like no one appreciates what you do. In fact, most of the time, they don't even notice at all. You need to be faithful.

Proverbs 20:6
"Most men will proclaim each his own goodness, but who can find a faithful man?"

Proverbs 25:19
"Confidence in an unfaithful man in time of trouble is like a bad tooth and a foot out of joint."

Solomon, the wisest man who ever lived, was responsible as God's king over God's people for the administration of God's kingdom on earth. He needed many helpers, supervisors, and leaders to work in God's kingdom. Even with all of his wisdom, he seemed to face a shortage of faithful men.

He did not have a shortage of those who could attest to their own accomplishments and gifts. There were plenty who would speak to their own worthiness. But faithful men were in short supply. Solomon heard their resumé with great hope, but when the work began or the challenges came he was sorely disappointed.

People haven't changed much in the 3,000 years since Solomon wrote the book of Proverbs. Faithfulness is a rare commodity. It is precisely this quality that leaders are looking for when they search for others to raise up. In this book we will seek to identify some of the challenges to faithfulness and some encouragement to pursue it in our own lives.

Let's begin by making a simple analysis of the word "faithful" in an effort to understand it. Our English word "faithful" is made up of a very religious word, "faith", and a very plain word, "full". The word "faithful" then, in English, would seem to refer to one who is full of faith. And that is surely true in one sense. The word is used in the Bible to describe those that are full of faith, believing and trusting God. But there is another quite remarkable way in which this word is used.

Surprisingly, this word is also used of the faith, trust or confidence that God can have *in us*. But that doesn't seem right. Even on our best day we would think that any trust God would have in us would be completely misplaced. He is the One who is trustworthy and faithful. Yet there are several characters in both the old and new testaments who are called "faithful". God told them what to do and they did it.

Jesus encouraged His disciples to live in the hope of one day hearing the words of their Master, "Well done, good and faithful servant." As He was approaching Jerusalem for the last time during His earthly ministry, excitement filled the air. Shortly, Jesus would be triumphantly riding from the Mount of Olives into the city on a donkey, heralded by the people as their Messiah and Deliverer.

But there was also a great misunderstanding among the people and even among Jesus' disciples as to the nature of His kingdom and how it would be established. Many were looking for the immediate deliverance from the Roman occupation and the establishment of a free Jewish state. But Jesus had a work to do upon the cross, bearing in His body the sins of the world in order to truly establish the kingdom of God in the hearts of people.

It was on this occasion that Jesus spoke what is commonly referred to as the parable of the talents. The parable is recorded in Matthew 25:14-30. The main point of the parable is that the master is going away but he will come back and settle accounts with those to whom he delegated resources and authority. The master is expecting a profit to be made. His servants are given resources and the master expects them to be faithful. He is entrusting them with His property. Of the three servants in the parable, two are commended with the words, "Well done, good and faithful servant!" The other servant is condemned. The difference is faithfulness.

Jesus told the story to clear up the misconception concerning the nature and establishment of His kingdom. But the parable conveys more than that. Jesus emphasized the idea that He trusted His servants. He would be "going away" and He expected His servants to be faithful. They would be stewards. He would be giving them His property and expecting them to be faithful with those resources.

In the parable, one of the servants proved to be unfaithful. He simply took what he had received and buried it away. When confronted upon the master's return, the servant said he was afraid of the master. He refers to the master as being "hard" or "exacting," placing the blame for his unfaithfulness on his master. His argument was that his inaction was justified by his fear. It was his master's fault that he didn't do anything. Jesus makes clear in the parable that the argument was unreasonable and merely an excuse. The man was rightly condemned for being unfaithful.

The unfaithful servant failed to recognize some basic concepts. First of all, he wasn't the master. He wasn't working at his own direction but was fulfilling someone else's wishes. Second, the property wasn't his. He was a steward. He would be returning the property to the rightful owner and was responsible to the owner for its condition. Third, while he had some understanding of the master's temperament, "you are a hard man," he failed to recognize the amazing generosity of his master. In Jesus' story, when the master settled his accounts he gave each servant a reward that was twice the amount they were accountable for. Fourth, the unfaithful servant didn't recognize the nature of the relationship he had with his master. Upon the master's return, he invites the faithful servants to: "enter into the joy of your lord". What servants in the ancient world (or the modern world for that matter) are invited into the joy of their lord? In the parable, Jesus is revolutionizing the master/servant relationship. According to Jesus, faithful service culminates in sharing the riches and glory of the master – *with* the master.

We have a tremendous opportunity as we serve Jesus. He is incredibly generous in entrusting His resources to us. He has many created beings that excel us in strength, glory, and beauty, and yet He has primarily entrusted the work of His kingdom on this earth to us. God believes in you and is calling you to serve Him.

We need to avoid making the same mistakes as the unfaithful servant. At first glance, the concepts seem so absolutely basic that no one could possibly neglect or fail to apply them. Yet Jesus told this parable to warn and alert us to the danger we face.

Many times servants forget they are actually servants. We become committed to our ministries. We see their importance and potential. We want them to grow. Sometimes we become so committed that we begin to think that they are "our" ministries. While it is important to have a sense of ownership, it shouldn't come at the expense of acknowledging the true owner.

God knows how to remind us that the ministry really belongs to Him. There is an old saying, "You know you are a servant by how you react when someone treats you like one." Most of the time, our service to Jesus involves serving His people. Most of the time God's people are very encouraging and supportive. But when our thinking begins to go astray, God will send people who actually treat us like we are their servants. We can become indignant and even angry at being taken for granted or being patronized. But in reality, this is just a wake up call. Whose servant are you? What are you really doing? Is this for Jesus or for you?

We have a Master and He has told us what to do. Jesus couldn't have been clearer in explaining the nature of His kingdom.

> Mark 9:35
> "And He sat down, called the twelve, and said to them, 'If anyone desires to be first, he shall be last of all and servant of all.'"
>
> Mark 10:42-45
> "But Jesus called them to Himself and said to them, 'You know that those who are considered rulers over the Gentiles lord it over them, and their great ones exercise authority over them. Yet it shall not be so among you; but whoever desires to become great among you shall be your servant. And whoever of you desires to be first shall be slave of all. For even the Son of Man did not come to be served, but to serve, and to give His life a ransom for many.'"

Jesus didn't come to be served but to serve. Service isn't the path to greatness. Service *is* greatness. To be last and least is to be first and best. Sometimes the competition for funds in the church budget or for the allocation of resources or for the timing and use of the multipurpose room can reveal that we have completely forgotten what Jesus said. We forget we are serving. We demand our way, becoming insistent that other ministries make way for ours. We forget that we have a master and we are doing His will.

So the question is, "What is my master telling me to do?" I don't have to waste any time with thoughts like, "Who are you to tell me to do that?" Or, "If you want it done, why don't you do it yourself!" Or, "You don't pay me enough to do that!"

Actually, I *am* being paid enough to do that. While the unfaithful servant failed to recognize the generosity of his master, we shouldn't. We will be rewarded upon His return. Sometimes our faithfulness is challenged by the perceived unfairness of our circumstances or by the actions of those in authority over us. Knowing that one day we will give an account to our master who has entrusted so much to us can help us get through these difficulties. One day soon we will see Him. We want to hear those words, "Well done, good and faithful servant."

Ultimately our service needs to be all about being with Jesus. In the final analysis, the unfaithful servant was unfaithful because he disregarded his master. He was focused on himself and how his service would affect him. We can be different from the unfaithful servant by keeping our eyes fixed on Jesus in all that we do.

Remember at the end of John the Baptist's life? He was in prison for taking a stand for what is right. He had been called by God to make straight the way of the Lord. The leadership of the nation, both politically and spiritually, was corrupt. John was faithful, taking a stand that put him at odds with both. His choice was difficult and painful and not without consequence. Herod imprisoned him because John had rightly called him out for his immoral relationship with Herodias, his brother's wife.

There in the prison, John was struggling to remember who Jesus really is and the exact nature of their relationship. He was sent to be the servant of the Lord. And he had been faithful. But things were bad and John was confused. He sent two of his disciples to Jesus to ask Him if He was really the One or should they look for another. Jesus' answer to John culminated in the statement, "Blessed is he who is not stumbled by Me."

Faithfulness doesn't make us immune to difficulty. Faithful service can lead to trouble, which in turn can lead to confusion. This seems to be what was happening to John. Maybe it has happened to you. You say, "Lord I did everything you told me to do and now these people in authority are against me," or "I've been faithful and yet the ministry is getting smaller! Where are You?"

We need to remember what the unfaithful servant failed to recognize about the nature of the relationship with his master. He thought his master was hard. He had no idea of the future the master had in store. Jesus said that when settling accounts, the master invited the faithful servants to enter into his joy. The servant/master relationship had been altered. The result of their faithful service was a joyful future with the master.

In his prison cell, John the Baptist seemed to be coming right to the edge of total discouragement. He was in a dark and lonely place, wondering if Jesus had forgotten him. Thankfully he reached out to Jesus for answers. The answer he received was a tough one, "Don't be stumbled by Me." Jesus was challenging John to trust Him, essentially saying, "Hang in there. Don't let this circumstance trouble you. Soon enough you will see that it was all worth it." Those who aren't stumbled by Jesus are always blessed.

It wasn't long after the servants returned with the message from Jesus, that the executioner came and took John from his cell. I can imagine him being led down the way to the place of death, his hands fastened behind his back and then being shoved down onto his knees. As strong arms forced his head down onto the chopping block, did he feel the wood against his face? I wonder what he thought. Maybe Jesus' words brought him comfort. Maybe he prayed, "Lord, even this doesn't stumble me. I don't understand but I love you and I trust you."

And they took his head.

And then he opened his eyes. There was Abraham. There were Moses and David. And Daniel. He had finished his race. Everything made sense now. Everyone was celebrating his triumphant finish. He had overcome and he was one of the heroes of the faith. Until the return of Jesus, faithful servants would find encouragement in his story. He hadn't failed at all even with his waning and weak faith.

John experienced what the unfaithful servant, a character in a parable that Jesus told, would never know. It's worth it. Faithfulness is worth it.

We are Jesus' servants, serving at His pleasure. We have been entrusted with His resources to do His will. He will reward us generously for our faithful service. But ultimately we are His children adopted into His family. We are His friends that He laid down His life for. He will bring us home and we'll be with Him forever.

2

Opportunity

The ability to recognize opportunities to serve is one of the necessary components of faithfulness. Yet so often we don't see the needs God is calling us to meet. Or we see something but don't realize that God is calling us to meet that need.

Solomon states in Proverbs 17:24,

> "Wisdom is in the sight of him who has understanding,
> But the eyes of a fool are on the ends of the earth."

According to Solomon, wisdom isn't far away at all but in fact is quite near. The fool however, cannot find wisdom. His eyes are in the ends of the earth. He is daydreaming of the far away. How tragic that he doesn't recognize what is right in front of him.

It can be the same with recognizing our opportunities. If my eyes are focused off in the distance at some far away ministry, then I will usually be blind to the need right in front of me. We can get fixated on what we might do someday, becoming so preoccupied with "someday" that we forget about today. We need wisdom from the Lord so we don't walk right past what God is calling us to do.

Remember in Luke 10:25- 37, the account of the lawyer who came to Jesus and asked Him what he needed to do to inherit eternal life? Jesus responded, "What is written in the law? What is your reading of it?"

The man responded by quoting the great commandment to love God with all your heart, soul, mind and strength and to love your neighbor as yourself.

Jesus then said, "Do this and you will live." But the man wanted to justify himself so he asked the infamous question, "Who is my neighbor?"

He was asking the wrong question. He knew what God's Word said. He is the one who stated the two great commandments, love God and love your neighbor. A much better question to ask Jesus would have been, "In light of what God has commanded, where and how can I get the kind of power I need to love God and my neighbor?" Jesus is ever ready to open our eyes to the needs all around us, fill us with His love, and give us power to meet those needs.

Not only did the man ask the wrong question, it was a dishonest one. As Luke points out, he asked it seeking to justify himself. It is as if he was saying, "I recognize there is a need but I don't know that I am required to meet it because the person may not be my neighbor."

The man must have been convicted by the words of Jesus. Perhaps as Jesus spoke, he thought of several instances when he ignored the need right in front of him. He knew that God's command was to love his neighbor. This man avoided opportunities to serve by excusing himself with the statement, "That isn't my neighbor."

Jesus answered his question with a story that we call the parable of the Good Samaritan. He contrasts the responses of three men to the same situation. All three see the same wounded man lying by the side of the road but only one responds to the need.

You have read in the parable a man is robbed, beaten and left for dead – a pretty horrific situation. He is lying on the ground, wounded, bloody and in great need. Then a priest comes by, sees the man but doesn't recognize his opportunity. Next, a Levite comes by, sees the man and doesn't recognize his opportunity. Then a Samaritan comes by, sees the man and stops and helps him. The lawyer had asked, "Who is my neighbor?" Jesus makes it pretty clear in the parable that anyone in need is our neighbor. We just need to recognize our opportunities.

In the parable, it is obvious that the priest and the Levite had an excellent opportunity to help someone in need. Jesus even describes that they saw the man and "passed by on the other side." The problem was not that they didn't see the man. They saw him just fine. They just didn't recognize that this was a chance for them to fulfill one of the great commands of God's law. They saw but didn't see.

If we see but don't see, then we will never be able to be faithful. I have watched this play out over and over. I was a janitor for several years at a large and effective church. God was touching many lives through the Bible teaching ministry of the pastor. Men would see the work God was doing and naturally want to be a part of it in a greater way. They would make an appointment with the assistant pastor to share their desire to be in the "ministry." When this would happen, the assistant pastor would say, "Come with me." Then he would march them back to the janitor closet and unceremoniously announce to me, "This man wants to be in the ministry. Put him in the ministry!"

Sometimes there would be a look of shock on their face since they weren't expecting to be brought to the janitor's closet but instead to the pastor's study. Sometimes they would zealously share of their heart to serve. I would usually say, "Follow me," and as we began to walk, I would ask them about the work Jesus was doing in their lives. They would tell me of how He had changed their lives and how they wanted to serve Him. It is always so encouraging to hear of how Jesus is working in people's hearts.

I would lead them to our back shop area and grab a push broom, a large shovel and a barrel. We would make our way to the curb that ran the couple hundred yards along the drainage ditch at the back end of the church property. The wind would blow all the leaves and garbage against that curb. It was a never-ending battle to keep that part of the church property looking nice.

I would say, "Welcome to the ministry. Use this broom and shovel and clean up this gutter. When you are done, come and find me and I'll give you some more ministry." Some of the men would say, "This isn't what I meant." I would encourage them with the words of Jesus that in His kingdom the greatest is the servant of all. Some guys would say, "Great. I'll come find you when I'm finished."

I knew that job would take about an hour or an hour and a half depending upon how fast and how thorough one worked. Usually at about the thirty-minute mark, I would go back and see how the newest addition to the ministry was doing. Each time I would find a broom, a shovel and a trash barrel but the minister was nowhere to be found!

What happened to faithfulness? I often wondered about the thought process as the decision was made to give up the project. Did he think he wasn't being taken seriously? When he said he wanted to be in the ministry, what did he mean? Was he thinking of teaching the thousands that met in the main sanctuary of the church? Why wasn't he able to see this need? The gutter was filled with leaves and windblown trash and surely needed to be cleaned. Why give up?

When Jesus washed His disciples feet, He was demonstrating that He was willing to humble Himself and perform the most menial job when the need called for it. He pointed out to them that in washing their feet, He was giving them an example to follow. They had each noticed the need but were unwilling to recognize that perhaps God wanted them to meet that need. Jesus said that as Master and Lord, He had no problem with meeting any need and neither should they.

I remember arriving early one Monday morning at the church and walking to the janitor closet to pick up the tools of my trade. I found someone waiting for me. He was rather excited or agitated, because he jumped up from where he was seated as I approached. "Come with me! I want to show you something," he commanded. Together we marched around the side of the main sanctuary.

We came to an outdoor planter that could also serve as a bench. There were several of these around the outside of the sanctuary and they were often used during the main services as overflow seating. He pointed to this dual-purpose planter and exclaimed, "Look at that!" It was immediately obvious to me what he was pointing at. The seating area of the planter was covered in bird dung! It was gross.

The man declared, "I am an usher here on Sundays. Yesterday people needed seats. But they couldn't sit here because of this bird dung. I wanted to make sure you saw this first thing this morning so you could clean it."

I was confused and I asked him why he didn't clean it yesterday when he first noticed it so that the people could sit down. His answer was, "I'm not the janitor. You are!" This man had an opportunity to serve that was right in front of him but somehow he missed it. He didn't think it was his job. He was an usher after all. I didn't mind cleaning up the mess. It was my job. But it was too late for the people who could have sat there on Sunday; and it was too late for my friend who had been given a great chance to serve the Lord and His people by making a place for them to hear the Word of God.

There are three basic responses to opportunities. The first response is to not notice the opportunity at all. In this case, the person doesn't care. He is not a servant. He wouldn't do anything even if you asked. The second response is seen in the person who doesn't notice the opportunity but will do something if he is asked. If unasked, he won't do anything. He is a "sort of" servant, always needing direction and never going the second mile. The third response is the best. This is the person who sees a need and meets it. This is the example that Jesus gave us. A good Biblical definition of a servant is someone who sees a need and meets it.

Too often people will see a need and then say something like, "I don't know why they don't do something about that!" Or, "They really should take care of this situation." Or, "They really should fix this!" Would you reread those statements and put the emphasis on the word, "they"? Early on in my ministry I wondered "Who is this magical group called 'they'"? It seemed they must be important for they are responsible to meet all the needs of the church! Then I realized a wonderful truth: I am "they." I am called to meet needs. When God shows us a need, most of the time He is calling us to meet it or at least be part of the solution.

It is true that I can't possibly meet every need in the world. Sometimes this fact paralyzes people. They can't do everything so they do nothing. The wisdom of Solomon's proverb is so helpful in this regard. God has something for me and it's right in front of me. I should not have my eyes in the ends of the earth, preoccupied with needs that I can't possibly meet, that God isn't calling me to meet, while I walk past the need right in front of me.

Paul writes in Galatians 6:10,

> "Therefore, as we have opportunity, let us do good to all, especially to those who are of the household of faith."

I am not responsible for the opportunities that I don't have. This is incredibly freeing. I can't do everything. Since I am not called to do everything, I don't have a heavy burden. Nor do I become overwhelmed by the tremendous work that needs to be done in the world. Everyday I can do what Jesus is calling me to do.

Remember that when rebuilding the walls of Jerusalem, Nehemiah assigned each family to a portion of the wall. No one person or family was responsible for the whole wall. The people had become discouraged and defeated looking at the whole project. It was so big and daunting and there were too many enemies and obstacles.

Are you facing this right now? So much needs to be done and there are so few workers committed to the task. The realization that you can't possibly do it all is setting in.

Nehemiah gave each family an opportunity to build. They would be responsible for only part of the wall. The key is that they heard from Nehemiah and they knew what portion was theirs. If each family faithfully built the section that was assigned to them then the wall would be finished. It *was* finished and in record time.

In the same way, Paul makes it clear that God will give me opportunities. What an incredible privilege to join with Jesus in what He is doing. Our world is in real trouble and needs a work of God. The needs are overwhelming, but God will show me opportunities to do good. I get to play a part in His great work! And so do you.

As you continue serving Jesus, ask Him to open your eyes to the needs right in front of you. Be careful not to let yourself get preoccupied with opportunities that really aren't yours. Be faithful to meet those needs that Jesus shows you. He will direct you. He will let you see some mess that needs cleaning. Remember that you are "they." The faithful servant is the one who sees a need and then meets it.

3

Whatever He Says to You

In the New Testament our service to Jesus is likened to several different occupations: fisherman, farmer, builder, shepherd, steward, etc. Fisherman fish. Farmers farm. Builders build. Shepherds shepherd. But what about the steward? Quite simply, the steward does what he is told. For the steward to be successful, he must be true to his master's will.

Paul writes in 1 Corinthians 4:2

> "Moreover it is required in stewards that one be found faithful."

Faithfulness is not an option, it is a requirement. The quality that the steward is seeking above all others is faithfulness. Let me remind you of the details surrounding the first miracle that Jesus performed, because it contains what might be the simplest picture of faithfulness in the Bible.

Jesus and His disciples were invited to a wedding. Mary the mother of Jesus was in attendance as well. The wedding took place in Cana of Galilee, which isn't too far from Nazareth. Apparently Mary was well acquainted with the hosts because as things at the reception went terribly wrong, she was immediately made aware of it.

The story of the miracle of the water turned into wine is a familiar one, but we can't let our familiarity with the story dull the edge of the drama as it unfolded. In many cultures, the requirement to show hospitality is paramount. To fail at this point would be the ultimate sign of disrespect and bring the highest degree of shame on the family.

Weddings are occasions of great joy for a bride and groom as well as their families, but they can also bring great stress even when everything goes smoothly. The unthinkable happened at this wedding in Cana: the hosts ran out of wine. In a moment, there would be nothing to serve the guests. Those that knew what was about to happen must have been panic-stricken. "What will we do?" "What will we say?" "How can we face everyone?" "Is there no solution?"

Mary comes to Jesus and tells Him what is happening. Perhaps something wasn't right in her heart as she spoke, for Jesus gently challenged her when He said, "Woman, what do I have to do with you? My hour has not yet come." He would act on His heavenly Father's terms and timing and no one else's, not even his mother's.

But Mary knew that Jesus would help, so she went and found the servants. Her words to them deliver the simplest and most straightforward statement about ministry ever spoken. She says, "Whatever He says to you, do it." Perfect advice. Many times we make ministry very complicated but it really is that simple. And faithfulness to that statement is what being a steward is all about.

Several important truths are implied in the command, "Whatever He says to you, do it." First, Jesus has a plan. Second, Jesus is willing to communicate that plan. Third, Jesus will use servants to accomplish His plan. Fourth, servants can be in a relationship with Jesus so that they can hear his voice and know His plan. Each of these truths is important in its own right and worthy of our consideration, but for our purposes, let's focus on the concept of faithfulness. What will Jesus command these servants to do? And will they do it?

Remember, the need is for more wine. They had served all the wine and nothing was left. Complete embarrassment and total panic is setting in. Behind the scenes, I am sure someone was blaming and someone was being blamed. The stress level is going up and there is little time to act before disaster strikes. Then Mary says to the servants, "Whatever He says to you, do it." The servants look at Jesus and He points to the six stone water pots set there for the purpose of purification. "Fill those water pots with water," He commands.

The need is for wine and not water. Notice that Jesus gives them a command to do something that won't bring them any closer to getting out of their predicament. I wonder if any of those servants was tempted to say something like, "Are you kidding? We don't have time to be messing around with that! We need wine, not water."

Even though Mary's statement is a very simple one, it can be difficult to obey. Jesus may command us to do something that doesn't make any sense. Has Jesus commanded you to do something that doesn't make sense? Have you obeyed Him yet? Or we may have come up with our own plan but then Jesus leads us in a different direction. Have you come up with your own plan but Jesus is leading you in a different direction? These situations are especially challenging when we are under pressure or things aren't going right.

The servants had to make a choice that day. It would have been easy to raise objections to what Jesus told them to do. They could have pointed out that they needed wine and not water. They might have been tempted to remind Jesus that water isn't wine. There was a sense of urgency and they didn't have time to waste. They could have said, "Thanks for the suggestion Jesus but we'll do something else." Or they could simply and faithfully do what He said.

In addition, Jesus was commanding them to do something that was a lot of work. Each of the stone water pots held around 20 or 30 gallons. They would need to fetch somewhere between 120 and 180 gallons of water. Have you ever carried a 5-gallon bucket of water? How many would it take to get 180 gallons? Remember, they don't have a municipal water supply pumping water under pressure to the wedding reception. They can't drag a water hose over and fill the pots. This water will most likely be coming out of a well, a well that is many feet deep. They will be hoisting this water up, out of the well and dragging it to the pots. How far away is the well? And at the end of all this hard labor, they won't have any wine, just a bunch of water. Seems like a lot of work to get nowhere.

Have you ever felt like you weren't getting anywhere even though you were doing exactly what Jesus told you? It is in times like this that we really learn what faithfulness is all about. When my efforts are immediately rewarded, it is "easy" to be faithful. But what about when there is no obvious connection between what I am doing and the positive results I hope to see? What about when my hard work isn't taking me forward, and from my perspective, even seems to be taking me backward? That is when I learn to be faithful.

We know how the story ends. We know that Jesus rescues the wedding from disaster, but don't forget that these servants didn't know how things were going to turn out. Their obedience to Jesus is a great illustration to us of the need to be faithful. Ministry really doesn't have to be more complicated than, "Whatever Jesus says to you, do it." They filled the water pots because He said to. No one had ever turned water into wine. It is impossible. It would take a miracle. And yet they did what Jesus said. And they left the results up to Him.

I love these servants. They are some of my personal heroes. Maybe they struggled with what He said. Maybe they didn't. The Bible doesn't give us that detail. But at some point something happened inside them and they decided to go for it. If you look carefully at the story, you will notice a detail that John points out: they filled the water pots up to the brim. In a sense the servants were saying, "Jesus, You said it. I don't really understand it. But I'm going for it! To the brim!"

You won't find a better example or picture of faithfulness in the Bible. Let me encourage you to be a "to the brim" kind of servant. When Jesus gives you direction or makes clear to you what He wants you to do, be faithful. Go for it. Do you know why they filled the water pots to the brim? Because you can't fill them anymore than that! They did exactly what Jesus said and they did it *all* the way.

We will consider this in more detail in another chapter but it's important to note that the servants will end up with as much wine as they have water. No more, no less. That's why it is so important that they filled the water pots to the brim. Remember Elisha, the widow and her son? Elisha told them to go and gather jars. The widow and the son went out and gathered an abundance. Every spare jar that could be found, they brought to Elisha. And all those jars were miraculously filled with oil! They would experience the miracle in proportion to the faith they expressed in obedience to the command of the prophet. That's why we need to be the "to the brim" kind of servants. Don't do your ministry halfway or half-hearted. Know that Jesus is working; He is about to do something amazing, so do your work "to the brim."

Imagine how these servants must look when they are done. Do they look like they have been working? Are they out of breath? Are they sweaty? Many times when Jesus is doing a miracle, servants can be found behind the scenes, tired and sweaty. Yes, Jesus does the miracle but by the grace of God, He lets us have a part in it! Is that you? No one else knows how much work is going on behind the scenes except for you, your fellow laborers, and of course Jesus. It was His idea in the first place and you have been faithful. There is great satisfaction and joy for tired, drenched-in-sweat servants who do what Jesus says!

There is more for us to learn from their experience, for Jesus gives them another command. And this command was more difficult to obey. It wouldn't be as physically challenging but would involve a greater step of faith. Jesus ordered, "Draw out some and take it to the head waiter."

This would be a problem. They still didn't have any wine, just 6 stone water pots filled with water. Yes, the water pots were filled to the brim but it was still water. All that hard work didn't make a miracle.

They still needed a miracle and we aren't told when it took place. Did all the water in the six water pots turn to wine immediately? Were there then six water pots filled with wine? That would make this pretty easy. The servants would draw out wine and take it to the waiter.

Or did the water turn into wine each time the servants drew it out and took it to the guests? Would they need another miracle each time they drew a pitcher-full? The Bible doesn't say when the miracle occurred and while we cannot say for sure, I have an opinion. In my life and in my experience, miracles happen in the moment at which I need them to happen. That is to say, I don't have 6 water pots filled with wine just sitting around waiting for me to draw it out. I usually have a pitcher full of water in my hand as I pray, "Jesus, You have done this before, please do it again. I need another miracle!" In my experience in service, I find myself continually looking for a fresh experience of Jesus' power. I want to encourage you to expect Jesus to bless your obedience. He told you what to do. You did it. Keep stepping out in faith and He will make the impossible happen.

While we can't say for sure when it happened, we do know what happened. Jesus changed the water into wine. When the headwaiter tasted it, he was amazed at its quality and told everyone so. He wasn't amazed at the miracle because he didn't know a miracle had taken place. He may not have even known how close the wedding reception was to disaster. But John points out that the servants knew. The servants knew what Jesus had done. While there was a great crowd enjoying the miracle, the faithful servants behind the scenes had seen Jesus perform His first miracle. They saw that He was someone who could change things from what they are and make them into something new.

This is often the case in ministry. There are many that enjoy the miracle of what Jesus has done but usually behind the scenes, there is a group of servants in awe of Jesus and what He just did. These servants know how close they came to disaster. They are aware of how desperately they needed Jesus to make the impossible happen. They literally got to watch the Lord work. Their appreciation and awareness of who Jesus is will grow as a result. The headwaiter praised the quality of the wine, but the servants who knew what happened praised the Winemaker. The place of service is often where Jesus reveals Himself in the most profound ways.

I want to encourage you who are working behind the scenes. Maybe a lot of your service is like the servants in this story and involves things like heavy stone water pots and dragging around buckets of water in the background. Maybe you are constantly in need of miracles. But they are behind-the-scenes miracles. Maybe your pastor or the elders will never even know. But you will. Whatever Jesus says to you, do it, and do it "to the brim." And you'll see Jesus.

4

Digging Ditches

> "For My thoughts are not your thoughts,
> Nor are your ways My ways," says the Lord.
>
> For as the heavens are higher than the earth,
> So are My ways higher than your ways,
> And My thoughts than your thoughts."
>
> Isaiah 55:8-9

Does God really need to emphasize that His ways and thoughts are infinitely above ours? Yes. We are prone to forget this most basic of truths. God knows the beginning from the end. We don't. His thoughts and ways are based on an understanding of things far beyond our grasp. It is vitally important for us then to learn to be faithful, doing exactly what God says.

Remember when Jesus asked Philip how much bread would be needed to feed the multitude? Jesus specifically asked him where they could buy it. Philip immediately calculated the daunting task and responded with a rough estimate of the cost of feeding such a group. Philip concluded that it was impossible. Jesus had said this to test him since He knew what He was about to do. He didn't need Philip's calculations, but He needed Philip to learn a great lesson: Jesus may do anything at any time, using just about anything or anyone, so you better pay attention and do what He says. Sometimes our own understanding of things can be the greatest enemy to our faithfulness.

Let me remind you of an event from Israel's history recorded in 2 Kings chapter 7. Jehoshaphat, king of Judah, was a good king. On one of his woefully misguided ventures with Jehoram, king of Israel, a great lesson in faithfulness plays out.

Jehoshaphat lived after Israel was divided into two kingdoms: the northern kingdom of Israel and the southern kingdom of Judah. As the king of Judah, his greatest failing was his infatuation with the wicked kings of the north. He spent lots of time with Ahab and Jezebel. He even took one of Ahab and Jezebel's daughters as a wife for his son, which led to great destruction later on.

Jehoshaphat continued this infatuation with Jehoram, who succeeded his father Ahab on the throne of the northern kingdom. As Israel turned away from the Lord and toward idols, God allowed difficulties to come to get the attention of the leaders and the people. The king of Moab rebelled against the tribute they had previously paid to Israel's northern kingdom. Jehoram decided to gather an army and deal with the tax revolt by force. He contacted the pagan king of Edom who agreed to join him. Surely there was loot to be taken and the king of Edom didn't mind sending a mercenary force. It wasn't his battle, but the chance for gain was too good to pass up.

Jehoram contacted Jehoshaphat with an explanation of the mercenary force and an invitation to join in the venture. Inexplicably Jehoshaphat responded, "I will go up. I am as you. My people as your people and my horses as your horses." So the godly king Jehoshaphat joined with Jehoram the backslidden king of Israel, and the pagan king of Edom. This ungodly alliance is a lesson in what not to do. But, God was about to do a work anyway.

Seven days into this mess, the reality that they had taken off without seeking God's will or direction set in. There was no water. No water for the men. No water for the animals. They had come too far to go back. There just wasn't enough water to make it back to the last water supply. They were dead where they stood. This is always the end of backsliding, by the way. It may take seven days, seven weeks or seven years, but there is always a bitter end of the road. And they were at the end of that road. In typical backslider fashion, Jehoram blamed God for their predicament saying, "God has called these three kings together to deliver them into the hand of the king of Moab!"

At this point, the story takes a turn, for Jehoshaphat was a king who sought the Lord (most of the time). He asked if there wasn't a prophet among them who could seek a word from God. By God's providence, Elisha the prophet had been traveling with them. And after rebuking their ungodly alliance, he gave them the word of the Lord.

Elisha tells them to dig ditches. In fact, he tells them to fill the valley with ditches. He tells them that even though they won't see rain or feel wind, God will fill that valley with water. And not only will God fill the valley with water but He will deliver the Moabites into their hands. They will defeat and spoil their enemies.

Quite a promise, but there was one big problem: they were dying of dehydration. They hadn't been at a water source in days. Their limited supplies were rapidly depleting and now they were near the end. Without a proper ration of water, they had surely grown weak. Common sense would say that they should conserve what little strength remained.

Instead God commands work, hard work. God commands work that would use up what little strength and water they had left.

Think about this for a moment. Have you ever dug a ditch? Have you ever spent all day digging ditches? Ditch-digging is sort of the standard for hard labor. It is backbreaking, exhausting and dirty work. God commanded them to dig and to fill the valley with ditches.

Have you ever been in a desert? Have you ever been on a hike in the desert? There is no shade, no escape from the suffocating heat. Even when there is a breeze it doesn't bring relief, but the feeling of being in a convection oven.

Now let's combine the two images and imagine digging ditches all day in the desert. Not exactly an easy thing to do even when we are at full strength. But that is exactly what God commanded! Laboring, without any shade, in the blazing heat with no water sounds like a recipe for disaster. Already exhausted and rationing their water, God calls his people to dig ditches in the hot sun. He promises that water will be coming even though they won't see it until it arrives.

Faithfulness is doing what God says. If God tells me to do something, will I do it? In the event we're considering, it would seem that God is commanding something that will actually speed up their death, not be the instrument of their salvation.

But, this is the point of the chapter. God knows what He is doing. He will tell us what to do. We obey. We may not understand at all and in fact, our common sense may be assaulted by God's command.

Proverbs 3:5-6 tells us:

> "Trust in the Lord with all your heart, and lean not on your own understanding; in all your ways acknowledge Him, and He shall direct your paths."

We are not to depend exclusively on our own understanding of things but look to God. He will make our way clear as we acknowledge Him. When God commands something that goes against our understanding, will we obey? Will we be faithful to do what God says when it looks like it might be the end of us?

Those that heard Elisha's command could be tempted to say, "We are digging our own graves. Water isn't coming out to this desert." "How can we use up our limited energy and water, with the enemy so close, on such a foolish idea? Dig ditches? You have got to be out of your mind!"

There will always be a battle in our minds as we seek to do God's will. In Isaiah 55:8-9, God pointed out the infinite gap between our thoughts and ways and His thoughts and ways. Bridging that gap and elevating our lives to bring them in line with God's direction usually involves struggle. The things of God are foolishness to the natural mind and we will have to accept this as we seek to faithfully obey God's commands for our life. We will be tempted to analyze and critique what God has said, as though we know what is really going on.

But we don't! Thank God that He does.

Those out in the desert on that day had a choice: do what God says or not. And in this case, they obeyed. They started digging. Digging in the hard, dry ground of the desert. Digging in hope or digging without hope, but digging in obedience. Wiping the sweat out of burning eyes, looking to the horizon but seeing no clouds, feeling no wind. There would be no storm in the desert on that day. Still digging. Finish one hole and begin another. By midday, the sun is beating down on an exhausted group of men as they continue digging. They dig ditches all through the day. And just as Elisha promised, no signs of storm or rain.

And just as Elisha also promised, the waters came by the next morning. They came from Edom. But how could that happen? You see, the day before as they were digging, somewhere up on the high plains of Edom, which rise in some places to over 5,000 feet, it had started raining. Miles away, far beyond the view of those dying men digging ditches, it was raining. The dry ground of the high plateau greedily drank in the much-needed water, quickly absorbing every drop. And it kept raining. Soon the ground was saturated and little puddles started forming. And it kept raining. Puddle joined puddle and soon little rivulets began to form as the water followed the pull of gravity. And it kept raining. Little rivulet joined little rivulet and now there was a little stream of water flowing, only a few inches wide. It kept raining. Now there were hundreds of little streams that soon joined to form a small river making its long way down to the desert floor.

The whole time they were digging, it was raining. They couldn't see it but the deliverance was already on its way. By the end of the day when they were exhausted, having used up the last bit of energy and perhaps last ration of water, a mighty river was making its way to them. It would soon arrive early in the morning.

If they started to dig once they saw the water, it would have been too late. Like so many flash floods in the desert, destruction would be the only effect. Instead, as they obeyed the command of God, they were preparing for God's provision. God knows the beginning from the end and He sees what we can't. We need to trust Him when He gives us direction. He will tell us what to do when we can't possibly see what is coming. Are you in a place where you don't quite understand why God has you doing what you are doing? Don't worry, He knows exactly what He has planned and soon enough you will too. Those that wait on the Lord will never be ashamed.

Early the next morning, the water from the rainfall that began so far away finally arrived. The words of the text are, "and water came by the way of Edom and filled the valley." The valley filled with all those empty ditches was now completely filled with water. There was more than enough water for them and all their animals. You can imagine how excited and thankful they were that they had obeyed God. Those ditches became their deliverance. They weren't digging their graves at all. The difference between a grave and a pool filled with water is the loving care and promise of an amazing God. And some crazy people who decided to do what God said.

The story doesn't end there. Those ditches filled with water created an unexpected view in the early morning light. Their enemy, the Moabite king, had marshaled his forces and was prepared to make an assault that very morning. His soldiers saw the reflected light of the sunrise on the pools of water and to them it looked like the valley was filled with blood. They quickly assumed that the confederation of the three kings had been broken and the armies turned on each other in the night and had massacred each other. The Moabite army rushed to what they thought was only spoil. Blinded by greed, no soldier wasted time arming himself for fear of missing out on taking a spoil of the dead armies. They charged headlong into a camp of armed soldiers, realizing too late their mistake, and were destroyed that day.

The obedience of the people of God to His command not only led to more than enough water, it also provided the means by which God delivered their enemy into their hands. No one could have known such a thing would happen. Except God.

When we seek God, He has promised to reveal Himself to us. And He has promised to direct us. We need to be faithful when He does, doing exactly what He said, in exactly the way He said to do it. God desires to work in ways that cause people to be in awe of Him. We need to overcome the temptation of relying on our own understanding when God has given us clear direction. When we are willing to obey, completely trusting the outcome to Him, He will glorify Himself through our lives. He desires for us to be part of things that only He could do.

Are you in a place where God has commanded you to do something that you don't understand? Remember that His ways aren't our ways. Has God given you a promise of deliverance? Trust Him. Are you faithfully obeying His command but there is no deliverance in sight? Let me encourage you that it is already raining. In the distance, beyond where you can see, it is already raining. Soon God will deliver. Fill the valley with ditches!

5

Letters from my Pastor

In a frame sitting prominently on my desk are four handwritten letters from my pastor to me. I received them during the years I was a janitor. There is a story behind each of these notes. If you look closely, you will notice that a couple of them are quite wrinkled. At first glance, you might think that when I read these notes the first time, I didn't like what they said, crumpled them up in anger, and threw them in the trash. You wouldn't be wrong. Each of these letters was a wakeup call to me as God was trying to help me learn to be faithful.

My pastor has had an amazing ministry and God has used him in wonderful ways. So, it's natural that a handwritten note from him would be a prized possession. In my case however, each of these notes is a note of correction. Today they serve as a reminder that I am serving Jesus and I need to do what He says, faithfully.

Let me explain. The first letter I received is written in pen on a piece of paper from the yellow legal pad that sat on the desk in the janitor closet. The letter says,

> "At 12:30 pm there were tissues on the floor of the men's restroom. At 6:15 pm they were still there. Please make sure this place is in tip top shape before you go."

My pastor had signed it. I found this letter sitting on the desk as I arrived early one Saturday morning. I became angry as I read it, saying to myself, "Look, if you want the trash picked up and you noticed it, then why didn't you pick it up?!" I thought to myself, "I don't like being treated like I am someone's servant!" I took that letter and wadded it up into a tight ball and threw it into the trash.

Then the Lord started to speak to me. I remembered that the day before I had noticed those very tissues on the floor of the men's bathroom. It was a Friday and Fridays were very busy at the church. We had a large women's ministry that met with about one thousand ladies in attendance. It was a lot of work to set everything up for them. I would arrive by six o'clock in the morning and work nonstop until they were gone at about noon. It could get hectic especially if something related to the facility went wrong. The women were great and I have so many memories of how God used that group of ladies. It was a privilege to serve them. Just take note that sometimes the ministry was challenging.

It was one of those days and when the last of the ladies had gone, it was time for me to eat lunch. I had food on my mind. I had just washed my hands in the bathroom and as I was walking out the door, I noticed this toilet paper on the floor in one of the stalls by a toilet. I distinctly remember having the thought, "You should pick that up right now." I also distinctly remember dismissing that thought by saying to myself, "I just washed my hands. That is toilet paper on the floor of a bathroom. I am really hungry. I am not picking that filthy paper up. I'll have to wash my hands again and I'm hungry. I'll do it later."

Then I had the very clear thought pop into my head, "You need to pick it up now. You will forget to do it later. Besides, it looks bad right now. Just do it." I didn't pay any attention to that thought. I just said to myself, "I'll get it later. I'm going to eat."

I forgot to pick it up later. I believe that it was God speaking to me and telling me what to do. I didn't listen. Within twenty minutes of me not listening, my pastor who had many more important things to do, came in and noticed the trash on the floor. I think God had him notice it because He was trying to teach me a lesson. And since I wouldn't listen to Jesus, He had my pastor notice that same trash again and offer me an encouraging word about my ministry.

I realized I had been caught. I was humbled. The Lord had told me what to do and I didn't do it. I was worried about getting my hands dirty. How could I ever be effective in ministry if I was unwilling to get my hands dirty? I was more interested in filling my stomach than in doing what Jesus said. I felt ashamed for the thoughts that I had about my pastor and the anger I felt. I pulled the crumpled note out of the trash can and tried to smooth the wrinkles out on the edge of the desk.

I wish I could say that this was the only letter I received. But it wasn't. Some time later, I received the second letter. It was sitting on the desk when I returned from lunch. The letter says,

> "Looks like someone lost lunch on the patio side of the main sanctuary."

I hope I don't offend anyone's sensibilities, but, "lost lunch" is another way of saying that someone vomited. As soon as I read this letter, I knew that I had done it again. I had seen that vomit on the ground as I was leaving for lunch. I had just washed my hands. This was all sounding so familiar to me. I had noticed what looked like vomit on the ground right next to the edge of a planter and I thought to myself, "That sure looks gross!" Then I had the thought, "You should clean that up right now so no one else has to see it. Go get a water hose and wash it away." I responded, "No, I just washed my hands. I am hungry. That is disgusting vomit. I want to go eat. I will clean it up later. Besides, there aren't a lot of people walking around on a Friday afternoon. Probably no one will see it. I'll clean it up as soon as I am done eating." My objections were met with the very clear thought, "Do it now." I said, "No."

I had only been gone at lunch for about 45 minutes but as soon as I got back, there was the note about the "lost lunch" on my desk. I asked the Lord, "Did you have my pastor walk out of his office and notice it as soon as I said, 'No'?" I realized that I hadn't listened to what Jesus was telling me to do again. I was humbled. I confessed to Him that I hadn't been faithful. I asked for help.

The third letter is written on a piece of paper towel from the dispenser in the men's restroom. It says,

"Men's room in fellowship hall is need of attention."

This letter is crumpled up as well. I was mad when I read it. The men's restroom in the fellowship hall was always in need of attention. We had a school on the property and the kids weren't allowed into the fellowship hall or the restrooms inside. For the most part the room would be used during the evenings and during the day, it would remain closed.

Except that several times a week, someone who had a key would use the fellowship hall restrooms and leave the outer door open. The school kids would go in and make a great mess of the place. They would throw paper towels all over the bathroom. I am sure it was a lot of fun for them but it made a lot of work for us. On this particular day, I saw the outer door of the fellowship hall open and I dreaded the thought of what the restrooms must look like. I went inside to discover that some kids had made a complete mess of the men's restroom. Wet paper towels and toilet paper were strewn all over the place.

I was pretty frustrated since we cleaned that bathroom everyday. We had already cleaned it that morning and now we were going to have to clean it again. I thought to myself, "If I clean this now, those kids will just get back in here somehow and make another mess. I am going to lock the outer doors of the fellowship hall and clean it up after school is over when the kids are gone."

Just then, the thought popped in my mind, "You should clean it now. Someone may need to use this bathroom. And it's a mess." I said, "People aren't supposed to be in here anyway. These kids are just going to trash it again. I don't like cleaning up the same mess over and over. I'll do it later." I had the very distinct thought, "Do it now." I didn't listen.

When I read that note on my desk, I knew exactly what that bathroom looked like. I didn't need my pastor to tell me. Jesus had already told me and I didn't listen. So, He sent my pastor to remind me. How would I ever be effective in serving Jesus if I was unwilling to clean up the same messes over and over again?

My problem was that I didn't like getting treated like a servant. Remember that saying, "You know you're a servant by how you react when someone treats you like one." I wasn't much of a servant. I resented having to clean up the same messes over and over. I was frustrated with the people who had continually left the doors unlocked. I felt justified in my own mind.

The problem was that Jesus had told me what to do and I disobeyed Him. He had called me to be His servant. I didn't really like being His servant. I needed to be humbled. I still needed to learn how to listen to His voice when He told me what to do. I picked that letter up out of the trash and tried to smooth the wrinkles out of it as well.

The fourth letter is the most embarrassing of all. I found it on the desk one day and when I read it, fear and dread filled my heart. I recognized immediately the handwriting of my pastor. There was a crude drawing of the placement of the wall-mounted urinals in the men's restroom. He had drawn an arrow pointing to one of them and the letter said, "This urinal not flushing properly."

I feared the worst for there was only one way he would have known that urinal wasn't flushing properly. You see, I knew there was something wrong with that urinal. I had noticed that it had a problem about a year earlier. There was a part that was made of pot metal and it was rotting away, slowly disintegrating bit by bit. That part was responsible for directing the water back against the urinal when the toilet was flushed. I noticed the flush was not right when I was cleaning it one day. The part was obsolete since the toilets were now several years old. I couldn't replace it but would need to fabricate a new one.

That would take time so I simply rotated the part and the water was now directed back against the urinal. But, I could only do this a few more times. So every couple of months, the part would disintegrate a little more and I would rotate it a little more. I knew this couldn't go on forever but I just didn't have the time to try to figure out how I would make a new one.

The day came when I rotated the metal to the last remaining part. I had the very clear thought, "You need to fix this now. You can't keep putting this off. This thing is going to completely disintegrate and whoever flushes this toilet will get showered with toilet water." I thought, "I don't have time to do this right now. I'll do it later." The words, "Do it now," popped into my head. I replied, "No, I won't forget. I'll do it later."

So when I saw that note on my desk, I knew exactly what it meant. I ran into the bathroom. I stood to the side of the urinal so I wouldn't get blasted. And even though I didn't want to know, I had to flush to see what would happen. I hit the handle and the water shot out of that flush valve in a great gush about four or five feet across the bathroom. Anyone who stood in front of that urinal and flushed it would have gotten soaked!

I fixed it that day. I never asked my pastor what happened. How did he know that urinal wasn't flushing properly? Had he been standing in front of it? Had I given my own dear pastor a shower from a urinal because I wouldn't listen to Jesus? I never mentioned it to him.

Years later I was sharing this same message on the importance of listening to Jesus with the junior high group from that church. My pastor was in the audience. God had directed me to share this message and I wasn't expecting my pastor to be there. When I found out that he was there, I was going to change the message. I didn't want to recount these stories in front of him. I was embarrassed. But most of all, I didn't want to find out what happened with that urinal. The Lord told me I needed to share. So I did.

Of course, all the junior high kids laughed a lot. And thankfully my pastor was laughing a lot too. When I told the story of the urinal, I mentioned that I never found out whether or not he got showered by it. When I was done speaking, a bunch of kids ran to him and I could overhear them asking, "Did the urinal water get on you?!?" Laughing, he replied, "All over me!"

What do you suppose the chances are that he would be the person who used the urinal the first time after that piece disintegrated? Would it have mattered who used it? I was responsible. Once again, I hadn't listened to what Jesus told me to do. How embarrassing.

I saved all those letters. They serve as a daily reminder to me that I need to do what Jesus says. If I listen to Him, He will tell me what to do. I just need to do it.

6

Faithful in Little

Did Jesus really make a cheating, lying man the main character of a parable? Yes He did. In fact, Jesus even interprets the meaning of the parable for us, making it clear that we should imitate the man – at least in one respect. The provocative tale of the steward who stole, recorded in Luke 16:1-13, is unique among the parables.

The steward was responsible for a rich man's property but he was squandering it. The master realized what was going on and told the steward that he would soon be fired from his job. Upon hearing that news, the steward knew he was in trouble. He had no interest in working hard or getting another job, so he quickly went around to those who owed his master money. He offered them a deal. He asked each one how much they owed and wrote them a new receipt cutting that amount in half. Thus, he was putting them in debt to him so to speak. Once he was fired, maybe one of them would help him. That's the story.

The steward wasn't good at his job. He was a thief and a liar, yet Jesus said that he was commended. He was commended because he used his present opportunity to prepare for his future. It is in that way and no other that his work is praised. Jesus said that in this respect the sons of this world are more shrewd than the sons of light. That is, the heathen recognize the need to use present opportunities more than the children of God.

Then Jesus brought forth two other lessons from the parable. In the context, He is teaching primarily about our relationship with money, but the principles extend beyond that application and can be applied more generally.

First of all, Jesus stated in Luke 16:10-11,

> "He who is faithful in what is least is faithful also in much; and he who is unjust in what is least is unjust also in much. Therefore if you have not been faithful in the unrighteous mammon, who will commit to your trust the true riches?"

Notice that He makes application specifically about our responsibility to be faithful with money. The steward in our story used money to prepare for his future. Now he did it in an immoral and ungodly way but he isn't commended for that. He is commended because he knew what was coming and so he acted. Jesus is teaching here that since we know what is coming we need to act. We can use the money that we have today to lay up our treasures in heaven. We only have a short time and then our opportunity will be gone, so we need to go for it.

But Jesus' statement, "he who is faithful in what is least is faithful also in much," can also be applied to the concept of faithfulness in a general way. Jesus is showing us how to recognize faithfulness. We will be able to see it in the little things. And here is where we can sometimes have a struggle.

Jesus will give us something to do. Lots of times it might be something that we perceive as small or insignificant, especially as we are beginning in our ministry. We may not be too excited; or if we are the excitement quickly wears off. We think that we are qualified for some duty that is more important. But Jesus hasn't opened a door for that. Instead, He is giving us an opportunity to learn faithfulness.

Will I be faithful with what God has given me to do or will I be lazy and distracted as I serve? Paul wrote to the servants in Colossians 3:23, "And whatever you do, do it heartily, as to the Lord and not to men." I am to do everything with a real passion and commitment. The only way to do that is if I am doing it for the Lord. He is the only one who can inspire that kind of devotion.

Let me give you another story from my own life. One day when I was a janitor, I was cleaning the men's bathroom. Because I was cleaning around the back of the toilet, I was looking from an angle that no one else would ever look from. I noticed a filthy area that was normally hidden away. It was tucked away in a corner between a stall support and a wall. It was obvious that no one could see this spot because it didn't look like anyone had ever cleaned it. It looked gross.

I had the thought, "You really should clean that." Now, I had learned the hard way how to recognize when God was speaking to me. I responded, "Lord, no one will ever see this. I have never seen this before and I'm the janitor. My pastor will never see this. The people will never see this." The Lord responded to me, "I see it. That's why I showed it to you. I want you to clean it. Do you work for your pastor or do you work for me?" I cleaned it.

Who do you work for? Who are you serving? I might be tempted to think that if I was given more meaningful work, then I might become more faithful. But, according to Jesus, that isn't true. Faithful with little is faithful with much. How do you serve when no one is looking? I have watched guys who were barely moving in one moment, jump into action in the next when they realized the pastor was nearby. That really shouldn't be the case if we are serving Jesus. He is always nearby.

Paul would write to Timothy about the deacons and their ministry in 1 Timothy 3:10:

> "But let these also first be tested; then let them serve as deacons, being found blameless."

The word "deacon" means "servant" as you know. The servants must first be tested. What kind of testing do they undergo? I would suggest that the most important aspect of service is faithfulness. Will they be faithful? How can we know? Give them something to do and see if they do it. Put them on probation. God put me on probation a long time ago and He hasn't taken me off!

The second lesson Jesus brought forth from the parable is in the statement in Luke 16:12:

> "And if you have not been faithful in what is another man's, who will give you what is your own?"

This is what we call a rhetorical question. A question is asked and the answer is implied. It is asked to get the listener to think about the answer. What is the answer to Jesus' question here? If I am not faithful with what belongs to someone else, who will give me my own? The answer is, no one will give me anything! I haven't demonstrated my faithfulness.

Do you have a desire to serve the Lord? Do you want to bring Him glory? Do you want to help people? Do you want to help them grow spiritually? Those are all good desires. Have you begun to do those things? Are you serving the Lord right now? Most likely, you are doing so by serving in someone else's ministry.

Most of us will spend our entire ministry being faithful in someone else's. Not many are called to be the pastor of a church or the leader of a ministry. Most of us will spend our lives supporting and serving the ministry of others and we are happy to do so.

I have seen some people who aren't so happy about that idea. They aspire to their own ministry. Paul wrote in 1 Timothy 3:1 that those who desire to be in a leadership role desire a good work. So the desire in and of itself isn't bad. The issue is that we need to learn faithfulness and demonstrate that faithfulness. We learn by serving in someone else's ministry.

The ministry never is mine. It isn't my Bible study, my church, my program or my anything. It is the Lord's. I can never let myself forget that. Serving someone else and their ministry is a way we can get that concept cemented in our mind.

Sometimes you won't like the way the leader is doing something. You might say to yourself, "If I were in charge, I wouldn't do it this way." Now, we can be tempted to complain, become lazy, or be distracted. Or worse. In times like these, we get to practice reminding ourselves that the ministry is the Lord's and we are serving Him. It might sound overly obvious but serving someone else is the best way to learn how not to serve yourself.

It is natural for us to be self-serving and self-seeking. We all struggle with this. We need to allow the Spirit of God to change our thinking and give us a new mind. Consider what the apostle Paul wrote about this in Philippians 2:3-5:

> "Let nothing be done through selfish ambition or conceit, but in lowliness of mind let each esteem others better than himself. Let each of you look

> out not only for his own interests, but also for the interests of others. Let this mind be in you which was also in Christ Jesus."

We need humility of mind or we will never be able to put others first. Thankfully, we receive this new mind from Jesus. We can adopt His way of thinking. Paul goes on to write about how Jesus emptied Himself and humbled Himself even submitting to the cross. Jesus was a servant. It is His very nature and essence. So, we also adopt that same humility of mind that is our Savior's.

But too often we don't; even those who are serving. Even Paul's own traveling companions and fellow servants. Look a few verses later in the same chapter in Philippians and read what Paul says:

> "But I trust in the Lord Jesus to send Timothy to you shortly, that I also may be encouraged when I know your state. For I have no one like-minded, who will sincerely care for your state. For all seek their own, not the things which are of Christ Jesus. But you know his proven character, that as a son with his father he served with me in the gospel."

Did you notice that Paul wrote that he had no one else he trusted to send to them? I often think of Paul and his companions as sort of Super Servants. They were always committed and never compromised. But that wasn't the case. I imagine Paul had a list of guys in his mind he could send to Philippi. It's not hard to imagine him going down that list, "No, I can't send him. He didn't do well the last time I sent him somewhere." Or, "I can't send him, he really seems preoccupied with how much support he has." Or, "When people look up to him, he just loves it too much. He'll take advantage of these folks."

As Paul thought about it, he only had one person he could send. Timothy. Notice what he said about him:

> "…you know his proven character, that as a son with his father he served with me in the gospel."

Paul knew what Timothy would do when he was by himself because he knew what Timothy did when he was with him. Timothy knew that the ministry wasn't his. He didn't seek his own. Some of the other guys hadn't learned that yet and so Paul didn't trust them. They hadn't been faithful when they were with him so how could he trust them out on their own?

If you want to have God give you more opportunity, then be faithful with the opportunities He has given you right now. If you want God to give you your own ministry then be faithful serving in someone else's; because the ministry is never your own. It's not your own even when it is your own! If I can't submit to the Lord in serving someone else, then I haven't truly learned that the ministry is God's and not man's.

This is where Paul's encouragement to do our work heartily as unto the Lord can really help us. Some of Paul's friends were seeking their own and not the things of Jesus. We have to keep it clear in our mind that the ministry is all the Lord's. If you are struggling with this, surrender. Fix your eyes on Jesus. He is the head of the church. Do what you do for Him. Trust Him and give it your all. Put your whole heart into serving Him faithfully, whatever He has given you to do. You won't regret it.

7

God Won't Forget

Have you ever felt like quitting? Ever asked yourself, "Why am I doing this? Is this even worth anything?" Even those who are faithful and have learned their lessons can still sometimes come to the end of the road. We can wonder what those faithful years of service were all about. Who were they for? What was the point?

We can lose sight of the big picture in the midst of our faithful service. It isn't hard to do. The writer to the Hebrews reminds us in chapter 6 verse 10 that even if we lose sight, God never will. He writes:

> "For God is not unjust to forget your work and labor of love which you have shown toward His name, in that you have ministered to the saints, and do minister."

The writer reminds us that God won't forget what we have done and are doing. Sometimes though, it can feel as if He has. We have been faithfully doing what He told us to do but our circumstances are screaming at us that God must have forgotten. This even happened to great Biblical heroes.

Elijah marched into the court of the wicked king Ahab and announced that there would be no rain in the land except at his word. Quite a bold move. I'm sure that at the beginning Ahab and his cronies mocked him saying, "Yeah right! It's not going to rain unless you say so! Haha!" But when it was dry through the first rainy season and then the second, Elijah would become Public Enemy Number One. He would become a hunted man.

But God had a plan to take care of him. He sent Elijah to hide out by the brook Cherith and promised to send ravens to bring him food. At the beginning it must have been quite exciting: Making a stand for God in the king's court. God was answering his prayer, there was no rain. He was drinking from the brook and eating what the birds brought to him.

But at some point the exhilaration must have worn off. The same drought that God brought to get the attention of the nation was also affecting Elijah. The brook that he was drinking from was getting smaller and smaller. With no rainfall, soon there would be no brook at all. I wonder if he built a small dam to try to keep the little water that was left. Ultimately the water would stop flowing, remaining only in muddy puddles. I wonder what he was thinking as he stooped to drink. Have you ever drunk from a puddle of muddy water?

I have also wondered what kind of food the birds brought him. I'm sure they didn't go by McDonalds and grab him a Big Mac and then fly it in. Have you ever seen birds eat? How do they feed their young? That's a gross thought isn't it? Have you ever seen the birds tearing the flesh from some roadkill? What are the birds bringing as the drought goes on? The Bible says they brought bread and meat. But it doesn't say what kind of bread and meat, or what condition they were in. His water is muddy and he is eating bird food. His initial amazement at God's provision must have given way to dread at the approaching calamity.

When we read the story, it simply says, "And the brook dried up." It doesn't say that God warned Elijah ahead of time. It doesn't say that he was reassured with the words, "Don't worry. I know what I am doing. I have a plan. This is what is happening next." Silence. God didn't say anything to him. Elijah just watched the brook dry up. Slowly but surely and little by little, the water stopped flowing. Did he begin to wonder if God forgot about him?

Have you ever gone through something like this? You have done what God told you to do. It was exciting but the excitement is gone and it's starting to look like He forgot you. Have you ever thought, "Did I miss something? Am I really doing what God said? Where is He?"

We don't know what Elijah was thinking. He doesn't tell us. No doubt it must have been a challenge as his only source of water dried up before his eyes. God didn't speak to him and lead him to what was next until after the brook dried up. Times like these test our faithfulness. Will we give up?

Elijah must have been relieved when God spoke to him and told Him that He had commanded a widow to take care of him. God sent him to her town to find her. He had been eating the food the birds brought him, but now he was heading to a home-cooked meal. If it were me, I would have been imagining the smell of the freshly baked bread from her oven. I would have been saying, "Thank you Lord for raising up a widow to provide food for me!"

When Elijah arrives at the town, he immediately meets a widow. Is she the one?!? God has led him directly to her! And she is gathering sticks. She is getting ready to cook! I would have been so excited. She probably has a whole spread at her house. She is the one!

Elijah approaches her and asks her for a cup of water. How thirsty he must have been. His brook dried up. The whole land is suffering. He is suffering. Now his deliverance is in sight. She brings him a cup of water. How refreshing it must have tasted. God has provided! No more muddy water and bird food.

He asks her for a morsel of bread. Listen to her response:

> "As the Lord your God lives, I do not have bread, only a handful of flour in a bin, and a little oil in a jar; and see, I am gathering a couple of sticks that

> I may go in and prepare it for myself and my son, that we may eat it, and die."

What would you have thought in that moment? I would have thought, "God you sent me to a widow who doesn't have any food?!? She is gathering sticks to eat and then die! What are You doing with my life?!?" Now we are referring to a Bible story. Sometimes we can read about these events without realizing that we are talking about real human beings who really lived through these things. This really happened. Elijah was a man who was just like us.

Have you ever gotten your hopes up that God was going to work in a certain way only to realize that He wasn't doing exactly what you thought? That is never easy. Proverbs 13:12 says, "Hope deferred makes the heart sick…" Can you imagine watching the brook dry up, praying and asking God for direction? The direction doesn't come until the brook is dry and then God leads you to a widow who is making her last meal so she and her son can die!

We don't read that Elijah struggled. Maybe he did. Maybe he didn't. How about me? How about you? Are we struggling with coming to grips with God's plan? Has He disappointed you? You have done exactly as He said but its not looking too good for you.

God didn't forget Elijah and He hasn't forgotten you. God used that "last supper" of the widow to feed her, her son, and Elijah until God brought the rain. They never had enough food to prepare more than one meal. But they only ate one meal at a time so they only needed one meal at a time. God's provision for him really was delivered through that widow who was about to die.

God cannot forget you because He isn't unjust. God rewards those who diligently seek Him. He knows exactly where you are. He sent you there. He hasn't forgotten you. He knows what you are doing for His people. And He knows that you are doing it for Him. He couldn't forget you!

The writer to the Hebrews goes on to say in verse 12,

> "...do not become sluggish, but imitate those who through faith and patience inherit the promises."

Faith and patience are required to make it all the way to the end. Many times our faith is strong. We know what God told us to do and we are doing it. Faithfully. But then as time goes on, we need patience to kick in. There isn't a need for patience until we have been at something for a while and things don't look promising. Then, we put patience into practice and remind ourselves of what God told us to do. And we keep doing it, the way He told us to do it, until He makes it clear we are to do something else.

Don't give up. It's too soon. Keep doing what He told you to do. He won't fail you and He hasn't forgotten you.

Of course God may direct us from one place of service to another. If He is directing you to move on to something else, to someplace else, then go for it. But most of the time, we don't need a new ministry just more patience.

The writer to the Hebrews tells us to "imitate those who through faith and patience inherit the promises." We have many examples of men and women who continued faithfully through "many dangers, toils and snares," and have found God's amazing grace.

In the New Testament, there are several faithful servants for us to imitate: Paul, Timothy, Tychicus, Epaphras, Onesimus, and Silas. They were faithful.

Think of how many times Paul might have been tempted to give up. Remember in 2 Timothy 4:9-16 where he describes how alone he was? Demas had abandoned him and the work. Several of the guys had been sent off on different missions. Only Luke was with him. He even says in 2 Timothy 4:16-17:

> "At my first defense no one stood with me, but all forsook me. May it not be charged against them. But the Lord stood with me..."

He had been forsaken by everyone! That is hard to imagine. How many of those who forsook him had been led to Christ through his ministry? Only to forsake him in a time of need. But the Lord stood with him. Paul found God when he couldn't find anyone else. God hadn't forsaken him. Jesus was right there and stood with him in all that he went through.

We already considered Timothy in a previous chapter. What about the names that aren't as familiar? Epaphras is called a faithful minister by Paul in Colossians 1:7. He is also called a fellow prisoner in Philemon 23. The faithful minister had become the fellow prisoner! Sometimes that happens. Doing God's will involves sacrifice and suffering.

Who is Tychicus? He is mentioned in several places in Paul's writings. Paul calls him a faithful servant in Ephesians 6:21 and Colossians 4:7. He is always on a mission when we read about him. He is traveling with Paul to Jerusalem in Acts 20. He was a man Paul could count on to send a message to a church. He sent Tychicus all over the Roman Empire!

Onesimus is called a faithful brother in Colossians 4:9 and was helpful to Paul in the ministry. We don't know much about him except that Paul trusted him to communicate with the church accurately all that God was doing.

And of course, there is Silas. We know a bit more about him. He also goes by the Latin form of his name, Silvanus. Peter considered him a faithful brother in 1 Peter 5:12. He was a traveling companion of Paul's. He is a great example to imitate. Remember when he and Paul had been beaten in Philippi and they were put in stocks in the prison? At midnight as they were singing praises to God, an earthquake came, the doors of the prison opened, and their chains fell off. You know the story. The jailor and his whole family got saved. He is a great example of one who through faith and patience inherited the promises.

God is at work in our lives and we are learning our lessons about faithfulness. Through the influence of the Spirit we actually become faithful. We are doing God's work with joy. People are blessed. God is blessed. We are blessed. But as time goes on, days turn into weeks, and weeks turn into years, we face a new challenge. We need long-term faithfulness. We need to hang in there when we've been doing the same thing for a long time. We don't want to lose our edge. Remember the message to those who are faithful? They will inherit the promises. May the Lord help us to be faithful, so that when we finish our race, we will hear those words, "Well done My good and faithful servant. Enter into the joy of your Lord!"